Cup of Home

Cup of Home

Poems by

Patricia Barnes

To Jan,

Enjoy!

Pat

11-25-19

Cover art: "Le Petit Dejeuner" by Patricia Barnes
Cover design by Shay Culligan

ISBN: 978-1-950462-42-1

Kelsay Books Inc.

kelsaybooks.com

502 S 1040 E, A119
American Fork, Utah 84003

Dedicated to Mary Patricia Sproat Barry
1916-2019

godmother, aunt, friend, travel companion

Acknowledgments

I'm grateful to the following publications in which these poems first appeared.

Alucinor: "Gem Eater" and "Wordless"

Encore: "Browsing"

Village of Acrobats: "Bijou," "Barred Windows," "Elephant," "House of My Childhood," "M'e Ntabising Drives a Stick Shift," "M'e Zim," "Postcard Home," "River Tour," "Tennessee," and "Your Money's Worth"

Water Music: "Laundromat"

Peninsula Poets: "The Bedroom, 1889," "Cup of Home," "Cuppa Joe," "Syrian Ashes," and "Browsing"

Sandcutter: "Frankie's Farewell" and "Widow"

Third Wednesday: "Drunk on Poetry," "Hard Luck Buttons," "My Study Is a Mess," and "Rust and Soot"

The following poems were First Place Award Winners:

"Aye Lassie," Utah State Poetry Society
"Bitter Loaf," Poetry Society of Michigan, (category: loss)
"Browsing," Illinois State Poetry Society
"Black and White Snapshot, 1951," Word and Sound Contest
"Barred Windows," Poetry Society of Michigan, (category: windows)
"Drunk on Poetry," Poetry Society of Michigan, (category: humor)
"Frankie's Farewell," Arizona State Contest
"Grandmother Wears One Shoe," Poetry Society of Michigan, (category: family)
"Laundromat," Poetry Society of Michigan, (category: Rumi)
"Pigeons on the Line," Poetry Society of Michigan, (category: nature)
"Singin' the Fat Blues," Poetry Society of Michigan, (category: humor)
"Syrian Ashes," Poetry Society of Michigan, (category: family)
"Widow," Arizona State Poetry Society, (category: death and dying)
"The Woman Who Was a Cemetery," Poetry Society of Michigan, (category: loss)

Contents

Part Two

Part One

On the Tip of My Tongue

I write slippery words,
ruffle-edged, fern-fringed, moon-freckled,
sassy with expectation,
words that sidle up to dreams
and poke nose-thumbing fun
at schedules and pie charts
without flavor,
itchy words that scratch
smooth surfaces and sandpaper away
the veneer of shoulds,
galloping words
too full of piss and vinegar
to stand still and have their syllables counted,
straining at the reins of punctuation
trampling commas with cloven hooves,
devilish words with the power of claiming
the ruby-throated hummingbird and the tsunami,
words as blue as old tattoos and saxophone riffs at midnight,
wild woman words, amazons, pole dancers, nuns,
words to make your eyes smart—
the smoke of campfires, peace pipes, funeral pyres,
drunken words slurred into laughter,
the language of mysticism and erotica,
words that last past my life,
words that drop with the solid thunk of a car door closing,
words hidden behind burqas,
lost as babies' teeth, trains of thought, innocence,
elusive as a fistful of mercury
or those lizards that skitter all over Florida,
words beating with rhythm's impulse,
the exhaled breath of an extended-phrase,
the romance of a monosyllabic sigh.
I want words that terrify—

saw-toothed, eerie, galumphing in the dark,
words that taste like baklava and are just as fattening,
words that dance tippy-toed
or Klondike stomping
or whirling dervishly into a trance
where it all makes sense
but still leaves you hungry
for one more bite, lick, mouthful
of words.

Syrian Ashes

The grandmothers' language was lies,
but all the children spoke cinnamon
and danced like whirligigs in rooms empty of echoes.

One grandmother ate olives and anger.
One burned sandalwood and memories.

Laughter belonged to another family,
but the children stole small pieces
and hid them in their pockets
along with ragged nightmares.

Olive grandmother found them
when she did laundry.
She gave them to sandalwood grandmother to burn.

Laundromat

This morning at the laundromat
I was reading Persian poetry,
in translation, of course,
I am without Farsi.
The drier tumbled comforters and socks.
Hafez tumbled Zoroastrian priests
with Moses and Jesus and Hallej,
who couldn't stop saying,
"I am the truth."
I watched through the transparent tondo
as purple and green
fabrics entwined and fell,
entwined and fell.
It was all so mystical,
the scent of softeners
sweet as incense—
and Persia, such a pretty word.
I thought—
fertile crescent,
Gilgamesh,
Mesopotamia—
I was dizzy with the beauty
of syllables,
the hypnotic swirl of the whirling
dervish laundry,
drying and drawing me
centuries, millennia
away from the laundromat.
Hafez had me by the heart.
He made music of the motor's hum,
the splash of rinse water,
the burble of agitation.
It was all one.

My Mezzo

My dragon can sing.
She is a mezzo-soprano
and favors the works of Rossini.

I was present once
when she accompanied herself
on the bass viol.

If you have never heard
a mezzo with a bass,
I tell you, the profundity is stirring.

My children do not believe
in singing dragons.
I regret that they are missing so much.

Perhaps when they grow up
they will be wise enough
to hear.

My Daughter's Shoelaces

I want your shoelace to tie itself into double knots,
so that you will not trip on what I have to say.

I want your shoelaces to wrap round and round
your ankles and calves,
so that you are a gladiator who isn't afraid of sharp words
against the skin of your heart.

I want your shoelaces to turn into jump ropes,
so that you and I can skip double-dutch
and never miss until lunchtime.

I want shoestrings just like yours
to lace energy back into my feet,
so that we can run together away from our nightmares
into a cool lake where we will float
even with our shoes on.

I want shoes without laces—
no shoes.
I want to walk barefoot with you
until we are all walked out,
all talked out,
until we can sit and breathe together,
and it will be enough.

Grandmother Wears One Shoe

She lives with broken things
and threadbare memory

raveled by clock ticks.
She believes in saving electricity

and pagan babies
but has forgotten why.

Someone ought to do the dishes.
Someone ought to unlock

the canisters of dry hope in her cupboard.
There are keys under every rug

and the combination to her safe
written in the margins of a cookbook.

She used to cook.
She used to read.

I remember a window box
with a red geranium.

The last time I saw her
she wore one shoe,

She thinks I stole the other.

The Darning Egg

There is a hole in my sock
right where my big toe curls up
and rubs the top of my shoe.

Grandma Sproat had a wooden darning egg
she slipped into threadbare stockings
in the evenings while we listened to the radio.
Cotton thread, double strands, in big-eyed needles,
don't ever let her catch you tying a knot.
"Weave it, dear, back and forth, back and forth, in and out.
No lumps."
She taught me to darn, damn.
With the fervor of preservationists
we reinforced all stress points,
toes, heels, and ankles
where bones rubbed work boots.

I wonder where that darning egg is nested.
Perhaps it sequesters with quilting hoops,
laundry bluing and pickle forks
in the neverland of wringer washers, hat pins
and hand-cranked ice cream makers.
They have attic chats of the days
when they were useful, admired,
state-of-the-art.

There is comfort in the solid feel
of a wooden egg in your hand.
It is dependable in its simplicity,
environmental in its inherent message,
and now nostalgic
as I look at the hole in my sock
and miss the simple frugality
my grandmother wore like a smile.

Cellar

10 Market Street
Seaforth, Ontario

Four huge cocoons down there.
No, four transparent, grey eggs
each contained the head of a ghost:
three women and a man, ancestors.

Shells cracked
and we took each other's measure.
We spoke,
a boon not granted to all who went down.

I do not know how they nodded,
being just heads,
but they did. When they closed their eyes,
it was time to leave.

You will say it was a dream.
But their warnings were wiser
than my imaginings, wiser than me.
Four pearly grey eggs of foreknowledge.

Out through the slanted, storm door
I eased into our weedy garden,
into sweet thistle and milkweed
scenting the summer yard.

First Communion

Saturday, May 5, 1948
10:00 A.M.

I am seven years old,
and having reached the age of reason,
am deemed capable of true sin,
both mortal and venial.
At my First Confession,
in preparation for what the nuns promise
will be the happiest day of my life,
I confess to being guilty of apostasy.
I like the sound of it, so serious,
worthy of absolution.
The priest snorts.
I blush in the dark of the confessional.
My penance is three Hail Marys,
and so I am shriven,
a clean vessel to receive
the consecrated host.

Saturday, May 5, 1948
7:00 P.M.

Mother unbraids my long pigtails
and washes my hair in the kitchen sink.
Grandma prepares a lemon rinse
(imagine the expense of lemons)
in honor of the occasion.
I weep as the two of them comb out tangles
and wrap long, wet snakes of hair
around rag strips, poor girls' curlers.
Pain before beauty, they coo.
I look in the mirror
and see Medusa, only I don't know her name.

Saturday, May 6, 1948
6:30 AM

I am dressed in a ruffled, white gown
trimmed with artificial lilies-of-the-valley,
a sign of my purity and readiness to receive
my Lord and my God
into my body.
I wear a veil.
I am a little bride of Jesus.
I have not had a drop of water since midnight.
There is no smell of breakfast in the house.
I keep my lips pressed tight together
in terror of accidently breaking my fast
and becoming ineligible
after all this.

Saturday, May 6, 1948
8:00 AM

I am at the end of the single file of girls
who process down the main aisle of St. Bridget's.
If the last shall be first in the Kingdom,
tall girls will be at the front of the line.
Oh, Lord, I am not worthy, we sing.
The air is filled with incense,
the scent of the beeswax altar candles,
the perfume of proud mothers,
and ushers' sweat.
I grip my rigid, white plastic bound, gold embossed
prayer book and I am grateful
for the pain of the rosary wound tight around my hand.

The sharp edges of little crystal beads dig into the space
between my thumb and pointer finger.
The hurt focuses me and keeps me from drifting
out of this perfectly prepared body
to Jesus in the mosaic dome.
His hand is raised,
gesturing for me to ascend with the incense,
perhaps he would give me a drink of water.
I rise.

Chalice

My teacup is chipped.
A delicate crack
like a river on a road map
traces a path to the handle.
I would throw the cup away,
but it was my mother's,
so even when empty of tea
it is full of memories.

I was not old enough to drink
from this cup
for a long time.

Take this cup
and drink from it.

Now I have held it,
drunk from it,
cracked it.

Mother, if it be possible,
let this cup pass from me.

I have swallowed the memories,
but I cannot empty the cup.

Invitation

She wrote a note
      to ten men,

dipped her pen in tea.   To me, she

        told literary tales
     lacy of metaphor,
     too long in the tooth to chew.

             But ten men strolled
to oolong,

        Darjeeling and pekoe.

It was the play of names
     and the steam scent of mountain groves,
     hand   picked leaves.

She wrote as small boats float
          with candles
   down
       the Ganges.

Her pen slipped,
     dancing
        sparse
            punctuation
on small squares of vellum,

vellum,
vellum,
       all true words.

The Bedroom, 1889

Dear Vincent,

    Forgive my boldness. You will think I am a voyeur, a loose woman if I say that I am attracted to your bed. But you must take part of the blame. If you had not let me in through the blue door, I would not have known the simple intensity of your most personal space.

    It may be that the actual bed is gray and the floor brown as your *Potato Eaters*. There may be old canvases and flattened paint tubes littering. If that is so, no one will know. Instead, we will always see the red blanket of passion barely in control.

    This is you, isn't it? This is another one of your self-portraits. It is your interior landscape, the vibrant, primary colors of true Van Gogh.

                            Gratefully,

This Man's Winter

Gray paint peeled from the front porch steps.
They would have to be scraped, sanded, primed again.

Winter was too close. Not enough time left.
He was at the end of his season for getting things done.

Snow would cover the eyesore.
Shoveling might slough off some chips—

if he shoveled. Waste of time to paint
before Spring. Waste of time. Waste of time.

The porch had once been bright blue,
matched to the front door and window frames.

Bright blue brought luck, everybody knew that
his wife had really believed it. She'd believed in him, too.

A mourning dove sat on the rusted swing set in the side yard.
Now and then, the wind gave a ghost child a push.

The man on the porch closed his eyes—
didn't care if he saw spring again.

The dove watched unblinkingly
and cooed to the empty swing.

Why My Hair Is Blue

I was baptized with powdered lapis
dissolved in wine.
My mother was the priest.

I was raised by dolphins in the Aegean
and frolicked with squid
whose ink was cerulean.

Blue hair is characteristic of women
who have wept an ocean of tears.
I have wept two oceans.

My hair is blue because it is my favorite color,
and life is too short to forgo
this simple, non-fattening indulgence.

My hair is not blue.
You are colorblind.

My hair is this color because I have prowled
for hours in Memphis,
soaking up the blues.

I am a devotee of an ancient offshoot of Ishtar's virgins.
We all have blue hair.

Blue hair is a symptom of a strange affliction
called azuritis. There is no cure.

This is a wig, I wish it were my hair.
This is my hair, I wish it were a wig.

Do you want to know why my eyes are green?

River Tour

Four seagulls sat on an ice floe
drifting down the Detroit River.
They looked like visitors on a river tour
gazing sometimes ahead
and sometimes at the shore,
taking it all in.

Look at that human, Mabel.
You don't see many of those
out this time of year.
Must be a wacko,
for god's sake don't squawk
and draw attention to yourself.

Mabel, beak high,
did not even turn her head
but continued downstream
as if she were the graceful prow
of a sleek schooner
bound for Lake Erie.

I watched their leisurely progress
and thought how pleasant
it would be to cruise
in a warmer current
on a Princess or Carnival floe.

Tennessee

It was my first trip into the mountains
where mist softens depth perception,
and black bears lurk comfortably.

A wild turkey and his dark
family showed themselves at the edge
of a path, past where visitors are common.

It was hard to breathe, hiking those damp trails
where age and altitude gifted me
with lightness of head and heart.

I felt the presence of creatures watching
and wanted nothing so much
as to belong in the silence.

Wrapped in translucent green
air that smelled of honest decay and hope,
I leaned hard on my walking stick.

What fallen log concealed a snake?
Which berries would poison hungry passers-by?

Now, as darkness hinted its approach,
which way was home, where a mug of coffee would warm
chilled fingers and soothe my throat?

Not that I had words to capture and express
late afternoon in Tennessee's true heart.
I turned to look for anything that would lead me home.

Barred Windows

All Peace Corps housing is barred,
so even the thatched rondavel
where my sister lives in the mountains
of Lesotho has bars
on the door and two narrow windows.
They are no barrier to puppies or rats,
but when the young men return
from initiation rites,
circumcised and full of testosterone,
ready for war and sex,
I am glad that my sister
is behind bars.
She is not afraid.
Only I,
nineteen air hours away,
lie awake and pray
that prayer is real.
My sister will leave her protective cage
to work with the AIDS orphans in the village,
the tubercular adults wrapped in their blankets,
the sangomas who seek to heal with herbs and spells.
In a few days the warriors
will be herd boys again,
their Bantu fighting sticks
will whack the bony rumps
of cattle on the way to find grass
or anything left to eat in this rocky place
of no water and few dreams.

M'e Zim is a Zulu nurse

She runs a clinic in Lesotho
for the Bantu people of the mountains
where there are no roads
and no medicines
except what she and the Peace Corps worker
scavenge and appropriate.

They are quite a team,
one short and dark and young,
the other tall and white-haired,
a grandmother.
Their smiles are identical.

The Peace Corps worker
has borrowed an old pick-up truck
to take a few who cannot walk
down the roadless mountain.
It is a bumpy ride
for fragile passengers.
They don't complain
just hold on to each other
on their way to M'e Zim.

When the clinic closes after a twelve-hour day,
she puts on rubber boots
and disinfects the place.
She will go to a village gathering tonight
to urge these people,
who are not her people,
to be tested for AIDS.
They will listen politely
to her waste-of-time ideas.
Life is difficult,
they do not want to know
they are dying.

Rust and Soot

Rust and soot were her wedding colors.

Iron oxide flakes floated like confetti onto the gaunt groom

and his hourly-waged wife as they exited

the furnace room of their nuptials

into the honeymoon factory of overtime and coffee breaks.

They had clocked in claiming no dependents

but punched out filing jointly.

At quitting time,

there was an impromptu reception in the parking lot—

vending machine catering.

The foreman lifted a toast from his hip flask.

The afternoon shift had chipped in for a gift

of matching safety goggles.

The bride wept at the symbolism.

The groom said thanks then started the pickup.

Someone had tied a worn work boot to the bumper.

It hopped along behind, the only dancer at the celebration.

Widow

After Tarzan died,
Jane swung independently
tree to tree
        and yodeled

soprano in the canopy.
Boy had gone off
to become Man.
        The eyrie

was quiet
except for the ambient
Muzak jungle provides.
        She wore

loincloths less skimpy,
more serviceable
and chose not
        to swim with crocodiles

but still bathed
beneath waterfalls
that had once seen
        erotic encounters.

Many animals kept
in touch, chattering
about the good old days
        before Tarzan

had trekked back
to the elephants' graveyard.
He had known it was his time,
        and she had let him go.

Leopards

Once a woman brought a man
two leopards on a leash.

He was sensibly terrified
and attracted to her exotic
lack of common sense.

Pleased with the rush of fear
she read on his face,
she put the leopards in a cage
next to his.

She lit a cigarette and laughed.

He longed to kiss
her crazy lips,
to wind her long hair
around his wrist.

Only the lack of a key
restrained him,
that, and the fear of leopards

who would begin to hunger
and purr against her ankles
before they tasted her beautiful blood.

They would let him watch.

Elephant

I would like to forget that elephant,
forget her undulating trunk
and embarrassment of a tail,
her both ends ropy,
marginally obscene.

I would prefer to remember
the Bengal tiger nursing her cubs,
regal, maternal, exquisitely sinister.
Ah, the pleasure of that frisson of fear.
I eyed her, carnivore to carnivore.

Or the Burmese python
casually coiled over a low-hanging limb,
one loop drooping
unconscious of its fall from grace,
as the extravagantly beautiful seem unaware
of full, flowing tresses as they recline.
Odalisque.

But no, I am ever in mind of the elephant,
delicately picking peanuts
from the hands of children
who proffer treats
through wide-spaced bars.
I hear her harrumph as she blows chaff
against my ankles, perhaps to catch my attention,
but I cannot look her in the eye.

Pets

She was five, and she wanted lots of pets,
so she drew a centipede

in pink chalk from the mailbox
to the garage with a zillion energetic

slashes for feet, and long antennae
ending in curlicues.

Then she skipped back and forth
along its spine, singing at the top of her lungs

until the edges faded,
and she went to get a drink of water

from the hose, just the thing
to give her pet a bath.

I think of that centipede soaking
into the grass with relief,

its dissolved particles draining past earthworms
in a mute warning

that they, too, could become pets.

Frankie's Farewell

My granddaughter formed an attachment
for a blue tetra fish, we kept
in a round bowl in the kitchen.
When the fancy fish floated
to the top of his limited world,
we held a solemn funeral.
The child took markers to decorate
a jewelry box for his casket.
She made a sign:
Here lyies Frankie RIP
We buried him in the garden
and sang "Three Little Fishies,"
the only fish song we all knew.
Then the child began to sing.
It was all about her good fish
and how she wished him well.
The facade of the quaint family ritual
cracked.
A quiet moment of true loss
touched us gently
as a gauzy fin.

So He Sang

My friend's mother died yesterday. The woman who had brought
him forth into this complexity of requirements and relationships
was gone. Now he was the eldest in the family. He would have to
start to behave. He did not cry in front of other people. No sir, he
had been a soldier, and some of the army's starch was left in his
spine; besides, it would not do for the grandchildren to see. So he
sang. It was a good old song from a church his mama had loved.
His song was his tears. The words covered her quiet face and
wrapped up her bones in the only embrace left to give.

M'e Ntabising* Drives a Stickshift

Mrs. Rejoice with Me

Her rented Toyota four-wheel drive
made roads where none had been before.
Herd boys, girl children, and chiefs,
donkeys and dogs watched the show,
but not those chickens of little faith
who refused to believe
in any miracles on their mountain.

M'e Ntabising was bringing an Afrikaner,
a geologist, to locate a water source
for the high, dry village of Menkhoaning.
Over the rocks and down the dongas
the pick-up truck climbed, slid, climbed again.

The good women of Menkhoaning
stood on stone outcroppings
ululating high and loud and joyful.
Get that white man up here, girl.

The man with the magnetometer,
GPS equipment and Ph.D.
would have preferred to drive,
but half-way down a donga is no place
to hand over the keys.
Besides, the lady behind the wheel
was having a fine time.
Her adrenaline accelerated
and so did the Toyota.

They reached a place level enough to park.
The geologist made the sign of the cross
and lugged his equipment out of the back.
M'e Ntabising got out, slammed the truck door
and danced.

Fathom

I have come to decipher the sea
to uncode the text of sand

see how my story is impressed
small shells punctuating

where gulls chase fog
where waves erase my passage

driftwood burns to smoke
a wisp
I chase it

I have come to write with water
to soak words into tides

see how my song is echoed
from cliffs of sharp stone

where gulls build
where hopes hatch

a soft grey blanket of sky
grace
I take it

Hard Luck Buttons

I spoke in hard luck buttons,
rags, and bones of a man's coat.
                —Sophia Rivkin

I heard quick stones of song,
morsels stale, no sweetness left.

I felt as eels and snails do,
my bones had gone to buttons.

I tasted every last scent
of old worries dipped in wine.

I knew why riddles bled
red, and why a matador's cape

is like Joseph's coat dancing.
My toes were cramped in rosy silk

slippers of memory,
all boneless rags of ballet.

Button my Loki lips
till lies come out my ears,

till I have forgotten the horseshoes,
the rabbits' feet, and all that clover.

Dune Tryst

We drank wine from shell cups,
you showed me how to eat
sweet, hidden bits of sea urchins.
I bit your shoulder
for the salt of it.

Our vow of silence
kept the peace
of erasing waves.

If you had asked me,
I would have stayed.
Neither of us dared
break the vow.

The sun dissolved,
sand cooled and drifted.
I was never there.

Drunk on Poetry

"For Li Po, it's a hundred poems per gallon of wine . . ."
"Song of the Eight Immortals in Wine"
—TuFu

When he wrote of blue-lotus roofs,
the Autumn River and the six-dragon sun,
when he flourished wild calligraphy across walls
and rejoiced in its beauty,
Li Po was drunk out of his gourd.

I have tried to follow
his profusely creative example,
but find that wine wipes out
my ability to spell,
and mornings after exercising
Li Po's writing rituals
my handiwork is as indecipherable
as Chinese characters,
rather mystical,
open to many interpretations.

I have lost something in translation
of the Li Po legend,
though as a cautionary tale
it serves me well.

I shall never try to dance
with the moon
while I am drunk
and in a boat.
Li Po did.
He drowned.

Part Two

House of My Childhood

The house said, "I recognize your footsteps."

I said, "You used to be bigger."

There was a moment of silence,
not a window blinked.
I sat on the porch.

"Have the old neighbors moved?" I asked.

"Look at the flowerbeds," the house replied,
purple impatiens and scarlet salvia,
Mrs. Harrison's perennial annuals,
familiar as the sound of a buzz saw
and the smell of sawdust
drifting from her husband's garage.

"Did you notice my new carport?"
It was aluminum and plexiglass.

"I'm sorry," I said.
"Pray for ivy."

"Buy me," the house creaked,
"restore me, fill me with your life."

"I have a new house now
in another town,
but it doesn't live in my dreams
the way you do."

A breeze caught the screen door,
it flapped against the siding
then banged shut.

Right Next Door

Inez lives alone.
She has not combed her hair
this year, can't bear to do it
because of migraines
that draw her drapes against the sun.
She retired twenty years ago
from her job as meat cutter at Kroger.
Our dogs adored her.
She would meet them at the fence with salami.
Dogs love salami.

When my son got married
in our backyard,
she painted her fence,
so it would look nice for the company.
When that same son died,
she left a tomato plant
on my front porch.

Inez does not like visitors in her house,
but if she sees me working in the yard
I can count on a long talk.
Inez is an indefatigable talker.
I smile and nod.
Every once in a while I say,
"really" or "no kidding."
She is suspicious of all the other neighbors.
She says they do bad things,
steal her packages, drink too much.
I invite her in for coffee,
but she never comes.

When I used to go on trips,
she would water my plants,
feed the dog, take in the mail.
She'd get all upset
if I brought her a thank-you gift.
"You don't owe me nothing," she'd say.
"I just do what neighbors do."

Last night an ambulance and two police cars
pulled into her driveway.
I would not have known
except for the red lights
flashing against my bedroom curtains.
I slipped my bare feet into boots,
pulled a parka over my nightgown,
and tromped through the snow
to find out what was going on.
She had fallen.

The ambulance took her to a hospital.
Today I went to see her.
I wondered if the nurses
would cut the knots
out of her hair. They didn't.
She still has her dreadlocks look.
She thinks she's been there for a long time.
She wants to go home.

I will want the same thing.

New Condo

new area code,
new zip,

no old echoes
bouncing past tense
from emptied rooms,

a short walk to the coney island,
long walk to church,

a stone's throw from the river,
three blocks from the tracks,

fog horns,
train whistles,
new harmonies, old songs
too much a part of me
to leave behind,

retractable awnings,
feral cats, a groundhog,
no memories in the paint.

View from a Higher Rung

We used to cut the grass,
but since we've moved up,
we mow our lawn.
I used to hire a kid to pull weeds,
now a landscape artist
takes care of all that.

Gone the days of going out for the mail
in curlers and robe.
Gone the backyard beer parties,
adieu dear keggers,
au revoir hot dogs on paper plates.
Bonjour marinated kebobs
and grilled vegetables.

I did not think I would miss yelling for the kids.
It isn't done here.
We text our offspring for dinner, and
the play date hostess drives them home.

Once gin rummy was our game,
but we've learned bridge, taken up tennis
and put away our bowling shoes.

My husband has a man cave.
I have a craft studio.
We no longer putz at the kitchen table together.

This is what we've always wanted.

Satan Speaks

And the devil said, "Let there be gluttony.
Let us make an overabundance available
and serve it with encouraging smiles
and flattery for the sinners' excellent choices.

Let us make it the fashion
to politely overindulge.
Let us make it an art,
a competition, a virtue
to get one's money's worth
at every all-you-can-eat opportunity.

The slightest nudge
towards a smorgasbord
will set them rolling,
course be course,
towards disability.

We will fatten them up
to the sizzling point,

and we will make dieting hell."

Fire-eater

I need to know the flavor of fire.
I need to swallow hell,

to incinerate the blasphemies and clever deceits
that spill so easily from these bright lips,

to immolate the falsehoods, I exhale.
I need to consume all that is corrupt,

to purify the language of flattery,
to tread the tightrope of martyrdom

stretched across my days.
I need to hear the crackle of salvation,

the roar of benediction,
to smell the char of purged temptation.

I need the taste and smoke of redemption,
the absolution of danger,
the blessing of fire.

Dreaded Diet

Do not pass me the salsa and the chips,
there is no power in me to say no,
and all the calories settle on my hips.

I must not let the nachos touch my lips,
for if I do my derriere will grow.
Do not pass me the salsa and the chips.

The magazines are full of diet tips,
they warn that every bite I take will show
and all the calories settle on my hips.

When I bend over, I hear seat-seam rips,
this means that I have had to learn to sew.
Do not pass me the salsa and the chips.

Cucumbers, carrots, celery but no dips,
I can't afford a treat because I know
that all the calories settle on my hips.

I've faced the facts and finally come to grips—
diet I must, but it's a bitter blow.
Do not pass me the salsa and the chips
for all the calories settle on my hips.

Epicurean's Lament

I love food, I don't deny it,
love to chew and taste and savor,
but alas, I'm on a diet.

Bake, sauté, steam, grill or fry it,
let me sample every flavor.
I love food, I don't deny it.

A new recipe? I'll try it.
Reading cookbooks makes me quiver,
but alas, I'm on a diet.

Hide the cake. Don't let me spy it
lest my firm resolve should waiver.
I love food, I don't deny it.

Must you crunch your chips? Be quiet!
Please do me this simple favor,
for alas, I'm on a diet.

Is there a weight-loss pill? I'll buy it.
What woman loves the girth life gave her?
I love food, I don't deny it,
but alas, I'm on a diet.

Ruminations on Lockjaw

Sometimes when I yawn,
my jaw cracks.
I experience a split-second of panic
as the word LOCKJAW flashes
in my mind.

My grandfather knew a man
whose jaw locked.
He never kissed his wife again.

I think of this when I am at the dentist,
my mouth full of fingers and tools.
What if I never get to swallow again?
What if I pass through life with my fillings exposed?
I'd be in permanent baby bird mode
waiting for the worm to drop.
I would have to pretend to be singing
so as not to look ridiculous.

Maybe, there's some kind of surgery.
Maybe they could remove my rigid jaw
and give me a bionic mandible,
so I could crack walnuts and
open beer bottles
with barely a grimace.

Now I remember why Grandpa told that story.
It was to talk me into a tetanus shot
after I stepped on that old strip of corrugated roofing,
I got the shot so I could grow up to be
a good kisser.

It is Love *in Absentia*

this bitter swallow closing my throat
with every missing breath.
It is a melody whose rhythm
is my heartbeat and the echo of his.
I inhale his name,
and breathe out the empty space.
Just when tears are exhausted,
I smell his scent on a stranger
and look for some new pain
to save me from drowning in the old.
So I float on the details of my day
borne up by small necessities
like a yoga on the nail points of reality.

Pigeons on the Line

Pigeons are warming their feet
on phone wires,
absorbing conversations
through their claws.

Feel the stimulating gossip,
the arrangement of trysts,
secrets skipping underfoot.

Black, feathered beads strung
against the 7 a.m. sky,
heads into winter,
tail feathers twitching for balance,
they tap into the babble of strangers.

Then, off they go
as if they'd heard something
so shocking
they couldn't stay on the line.

They flutter,
swirl
and reassemble,
drawn by curiosity
or camaraderie
to listen for more.

Curious Gift

I bought a bottle of curiosity
as a gift for my apathetic niece.
She has everything else.

The tonic was carbonated
and dandelion yellow.

I looked for a warning on the label like:
Do not give to cats.
I checked to see if there was a dosage
not to exceed.
There was a list of possible side effects,
but the print was too small to read.

I paid full price.

On the way home,
the bag on the car seat next to me
gave off a small hum,
like what's left after a bell rings.
It made my eardrums tingle.

I wondered how it smelled,
if the flavor was citrusy, clovish or sour.
The bottle had a screw cap.
My niece would never know
if I took a sniff, a sip.

No, no, no.
I'll wrap it right away
as soon as I get home.

I am a person of good intention.
It did not taste like citrus or cloves.
It was salty and smelled like a promise.
It made me thirsty for just another little sip.

As I pulled into my driveway,
I marveled at the power of tiny sips
to empty a bottle.

Aye, Lassie

Some call me thrifty, others say frugal,
those who don't like me say cheap.
In the lowlands of Scotland, my loved ones are buried,
they smile as they sleep the big sleep.

Uncles Oscar and Philly and dear Uncle Hugh
would say, "Aye Lassie" and approve what I do.
Aunts Barbara and Jenny, sweet Jeanie and Ruth
would wave with their aprons because it's the truth.

For I save my money and try to live sparing.
Just like the whole family, I mend what I'm wearing.
What's simple is plenty, believe it or not,
I value the wee things because I'm a Scot.

My Career in Sales

Uncle Walter owned a trailer lot
on the Eastside of Detroit.
Every year right after Thanksgiving
his half acre of blacktop was transformed
into an urban woods.
Hundreds and hundreds
of Scotch pines, balsams and spruce trees
leaned against the dark green slats of his trailers,
and I became a Christmas tree seller.
I was twelve and a half
and got a fifty-cent commission
on every tree I sold.
Big money,
as much as I'd make for an hour of babysitting,
so sometimes I put on a little pressure,
especially with the men.
Uncle Walter knew what he was doing.
Those Eastside guys were suckers
for little girls pushing Christmas trees.
Oh, the joy,
of putting Uncle Walter's two dollars
in the metal cash box
and slipping my fifty cents
into my snow pants' pocket.
I loved to hear the quarters clink
as I walked from tree to tree
pointing out the fullness of the scotch pines,
the pungent scent of the balsams.
"Your kids would love this one, sir."
They fell for that line every time.
Clink, clink.
The last tree I sold
was to a man who didn't want one.
He had come to rent a trailer,

but he left with a nice spruce.
I watched him drag it to his car
and throw it into his trunk.
"Hey, mister," I called,
but he slammed the car door and drove away.
I told Uncle Walter I was going home for lunch,
but I never came back.

Thanksgiving Traditions

The other kids pulled day-old bread into chunks,
I chopped onions until I cried.
Good turkey stuffing is seasoned with sage and tears.

Most of the family prefer cranberry jelly
served in the shape of the can,
but an in-law brings her homemade lumpy stuff
hiding nasty bits of orange rind.
We pass it around as if we like it.

When I was old enough to baste the turkey,
I felt I should get to eat at the grown-ups' table.
After all, I had met the challenges:
hot oven racks and sizzling drippings.
Grandma watched and nodded.
Still, I was assigned to the folding table
set up for the kids.

Turned out it was no judgment on my maturity,
only a matter of the limited number
of fine china place settings.
When somebody dies, I'll move up.
I'm trying not to think of anyone in particular.
It's hard.

Uncle Stan

You are dead,
so I can say anything I want
about how you scared me
with the way you yelled.
I am yelling this at you.
I am saying little girls should not
have to hear
big men yell at their wives.

So maybe you would say
you weren't yelling at me
so I should shut up.
But see how you say shut up.
That is not what you should say
to a little girl
visiting her darling aunt
and scary uncle.

How could you yell at her?
All she did was take care of you,
cook your dinners, iron your shirts,
keep your shoes polished with her own spit.

I heard
the loud, bad words,
saw you raise your hand.
I covered my ears
but couldn't run.

So, years later
when I got the news,
I knew why
she had hanged herself in her closet.
It was the yelling, and
it was because I had heard.

Cousin LeRoy Brings Grandma Back

I asked him if he was going
to dress up for Halloween.

LeRoy screwed his eighty-seven-year-old face
into a grimace
and lost a few grits out of the side of his mouth,
"This here is my false face," he said.
It was pretty scary,
what with the grits and all.

LeRoy calls grits "Georgia ice cream,"
and orders them every time
we go out for breakfast.
He gave me a bite once,
it took a while to swallow.

"Swaller" is how Grandma said that word.
It had a diminutive sound
with an echo of Appalachia
and the feel of her quilted bedspread
where I would lie and listen
to her read the Bible
with hill music in every word
and faith to move mountains
at her callused fingertips.

Sacramental Radio

Last Sunday morning, when I opened the back door,
I was surprised to hear our neighborhood had music.
This is a quiet section of town, especially sleepy
or churchgoing on the first day of the week.
Who had the verve to turn on a radio?
It was an unusual public display of presence.

I was delighted with this robust and honest presence
which came from my neighbor's open garage door.
He was sorting tools and listening to the radio.
I was impressed with his choice of music,
you don't find Mahler outdoors every day of the week.
I admit that in concert halls he sometimes makes me sleepy,

but on this crisp April morning, who could be sleepy,
swept into the maestro's dramatic presence?
What a powerful way to begin the week!
I breathed in the glory coming through my open door
grateful for the pain and pomp of music,
grateful for the excellent speakers of my neighbor's radio.

I went inside to turn on my own radio.
This was no morning to be dull and sleepy.
I needed the fresh transformation of music,
I needed to worship in the deity's symphonic presence.
Was heaven's gate as close as my back door?
I'd pray at home instead of church this week.

On that, the first day, I foresaw a week
when every day began with my radio
serving as a celestial door.
I'd wake to trumpets and tympanies. Who's sleepy
in their glorious crescendo of presence?

The salvation of my tomorrow's lay in music.
Perhaps I counted too hard on the power of music,
because after the sincerest trial of one week
I did not every day experience the presence
of divinity coming from my radio.
I admit to often feeling sleepy
and unresponsive to its knock on my soul's door.

It was not enough to be in the presence of splendid music,
although it provided a door through which I could face the week.
A sacramental radio cannot raise the spirit of those whose mortal
flesh is just too sleepy.

Scrupula

Upon genuflecting next to Sunday's pew,
my bare knee encountered a grain of rice,
unswept, singular, small as a *scrupulous,*
leftover from Saturday's wedding.
I swore,
Oh, Jesus,
and wept one tear
for my arthritic knee.
The woman in front of me
bowed her head in reverence
for the holy name
I'd uttered in spontaneous prayer.
She turned and bestowed an edified smile.
I grimaced, rose
and kicked the rice under a kneeler.
It rolled
to where a fasting nun
picked it up with the tip
of her moistened finger
and ate it.
Oh, Jesus.

Knees

I have been knee-deep in laundry,
Queen Anne's lace
and trouble.
I have kneed a too ardent wooer
and needed to woo with ardor.
I have knelt to pray
and prayed to rise from kneeling.
All those years of genuflecting,
scrubbing linoleum,
waging the weed wars,
all those squats,
not to please a personal trainer, but
to eyeball a toddler,
pee in the woods,
or retrieve lightening-frightened children
from under beds
have taken their toll,
my patellae have paid the price.
My knees rebel against stilettos
and stairways.
They creak when I stand,
protest the damp
and speak to me of weather patterns.
Several friends have had theirs replaced,
but I am too attached to mine
and would hardly trust novice knees
to dandle my granddaughter
or remember to curtsy
should the queen drop in.
One never knows
when a good old joint
will be needed.

Knock, Knock

Who's There?
Just Me Rappin'

I rub 'em in, I swallow 'em down
even inject 'em without a frown
cause it's old or dead—
I take my meds.

Remember this about Eliquis
it keeps blood flowin'
no damn clots goin'
to the lungs or brain
cause a stroke's a strain
on independent livin'
and the peace it's givin'
to take care of yourself
not stuck on the shelf, out of the way
cause you've had your day.

Cholesterol, a plaque attack
could set me back, so I keep track
of my HDL and LDL what the hell.
Lovastatin keeps my numbers low
'cause I just ain't ready to go.

Osteoporosis? Let me take
a calcium pill so my bones won't break,
don't put me there in that wheelchair
I need another chance to dance.

Pass the fish oil, pass the Tums
pass the floss to save my gums.
Baby aspirin does the trick
to help my aging ticker tick.

Arthritis is a bane,
makes me stiff, gives me pain
but Advil drives that devil out,
plus it even works on gout.

I rub 'em in, I swallow 'em down
even inject 'em without a frown
cause it's old or dead—
I take my meds.

Cuppa Joe

Java, like lava
erupting into the morning.
A fix, a hit
and all so legal.
Percolate, percolate, percolate. Pour
into a pottery, Styrofoam or bone china
vessel of wakefulness.

Tiny Turkish cups
turn upside down
so the dregs will run into patterns
a seer can read,
grounds for decisions
where to travel
when to marry
from whom to run.

The aroma of Kenyan coffee beans
roasted to the color of the hands
that picked them.
Taste their trouble.
Swallow their darkness.

Filter the flavor
through sipping lips
as you sit in your kitchen
inhaling the exotic.
Touch with your tongue
the mystery of coffee.

Browsing

I sit in Border's sipping a chai latte
and looking for large ladies.
This all began with the gift certificate
smoldering in my purse,
but I wanted all the books.
Look at that, her butt crack is showing.
I tried the music section,
but I needed everything there,
so I grazed among the greeting cards and
finally bought a latte.
It's very good, so it must be fattening
that's why I started seeking solace
in the community of the corpulent
where X is a size, not a rating.
I have assumed the persona of a Rubens' model,
maybe a Titian-type temptress,
ample, abundant, ripe as a rosy apple.
Damn, this latte is good.
I am definitely perking up,
though *perky* is not a word
we full-figured women take to ourselves,
and please don't even think *jolly*.
Buddha-like is also off the list.
I cannot even cross my knees,
let alone assume the lotus.
Honey, that tattoo is not a big enough distraction.
I like the sound of *statuesque*
and *Earth Mother* is appropriate
because it encompasses my summer wardrobe
of tie-dyed tent dresses, but
goddess is no good,
too many images of those prehistoric
fertility figurines,
big hips, no heads.

No, no, not horizontal stripes. What is she thinking?
I rest the latte on my bosom,
brush off the crumbs—
did I forget to mention the butter brickle scone?
Here comes Baby Cakes, the Queen of the World,
poetry in motion,
the ripple of her wake lifts me,
and I drift out of Borders.

Gem Eater

She slipped the ruby between her lips
and tasted Taj Mahal,
all Indian spices wrapped
like sari silk around her sorrows,
and she wept them away.

She bit the emerald lightly,
nibbled Colombian rain forest,
fed on green so dense,
only the cold stone could capture
and free one refraction of light,
the secret flavor of yesterday.

Tiny diamonds
sprinkled on her tongue,
a frost of forgetfulness,
crystalline calm.
She swallowed.

Muse

You eat every bite I have to say
and smack your lips,
lick the crumbs from the down-turned corners
of your ever-hungry mouth.

I can never satisfy you,
no matter how I sing us into being,
whistling words into spirit,
finding flesh for our bones.

Your hollow heart draws
my dreams from the dark
to fragment then dissolves
like sugar in your tea.

You drink them down
and I am bereft of fantasies,
empty again and scrambling
for a thought to sustain me.

I would send you away
if I thought I could survive
without an audience.

The Ache

I am extracting,
without Novocaine,
the root of this impacted reality.
Skip the nitrous oxide of sissies,
it is no laughing matter,
this probing of tender tissue
swollen with the promise
of an insight and the word for it.
One needs a mirror to do this
reaching into self, reflecting
and pulling until the pop
of freedom.
Rinse and spit.
Oh, the relief of words on paper,
a bloody business
this poetry.

Untitled

after Earth and Green
—Mark Rothko, 1955

Abstraction

is a lot like extraction,

you pull something out
                    to get to the root.

            Numbing is not involved
in the process,

only in effect.

Metaphysics is like that
            so is Rothko's art,

but with Rothko there is color.

            Thank God for the color.

And the best part is that he,

            Rothko, not God,
        puts it in interesting places.

No criticism of God's palette,

you can't top dawn or the sky before a tornado.

But there you have a hint of what's coming,

            in abstraction, you don't.

83

Up, Up and Away

When my brother was five
he believed he was Superman,
so he safety-pinned a beach towel
around his neck and jumped
off the second floor landing.

I often dream that I can fly,
breaststroke through the air,
rise with an inhalation,
steer with graceful twists
of the wrist.

My brother knocked out his front teeth,
mostly baby teeth
so it didn't much matter,
but there was a lot of blood.
We used his super cape to wipe up.

I have read of saints
with the gift of levitation,
the grace of anti-gravity.
I would like to be less grave,
less burdened with *gravitas*.

My brother has found other ways
to take off, though many landings
have been rough, and there has been more blood.
He has not given up on perfecting flight.
I am counting on him.

Leftover Turkey

On Thanksgiving day 1957,
my four-year-old brother
brought home a stray dog,
a small, brown mongrel with big, sad eyes.
Our mother (and I don't know how this happened
it was like some kind of miracle or something)
said he could keep it and give it a name.
My brother looked around the busy kitchen,
saw the sweet potato soufflé, the pumpkin pies,
the Waldorf salad, and the golden-skinned,
twenty-pound bird Grandma was basting.
His name is Turkey, my brother said,
and that was that.

Benjamin Franklin proposed that the turkey
should be our national bird,
instead, we got the eagle, a bird of prey.
How different our national character might have been
with a gobbler on the presidential seal.

Can you imagine how embarrassing it was
for me, a self-conscious adolescent,
to have to call the dog?
Here Turkey, here Turkey.
Or on a walk, *Heel Turkey, sit boy.*

I breathed a sigh of relief when Turkey ran away.
I imagined another family falling for those mournful eyes,
and wondered what they named him.
I've read that Dr. Oz is of Turkish descent.
If he has a dog, what's its name?
Probably Tofu or Soy Bean or Broccoli.

My brother recovered from the loss of his mutt
and threw himself into collecting earthworms
which he named after his sisters.
Last week I received some junk mail from a travel agency:
Visit Istanbul. Cruise the Bosporus.
All the old Turkey memories trotted back.

I sit in Heritage Park, watching people walk their dogs.
I hear, *Come, Rosalind, Good boy Titus, Heel Belvedere,*
and think of my brother's simple choice
to name his stinky stray after what smelled good.

Sirius

When the greyhound took Best of Show,
I thought, there goes an Audrey Hepburn of a dog,
the minimalization of haute couture,
the soul of grace.

We used to have dogs,
but vet bills went through the roof,
then the dogs died anyway.
No, we killed them,
put them down,
paid a professional to do the deed.

So what do you think about mercy killing,
euthanasia,
abortion,
capital punishment?

There was a close-up of the greyhound's face.
Her elegant eyes—limpid pools of ignorance.
I envied the dog.
I envied the dog.

The Woman Who Was a Cemetery

To scatter ashes was the trendy thing.
Release them into the air.
Free them. Be free.
But it was more than she could bear.

Where would they be then,
wisps of what had been,
fading, silvering out?

So she luggaged them home to home

and did not speak of the contents
of those two ebony boxes,
just set them where she could touch
in passing
what was.

Alley Psalm

When I walked through the alleys
of my childhood
evil had no safe place.

I threw smooth stones at garbage cans
for the glory of clatter and
to proclaim the trueness of my aim.

Broken glass sparkled,
the gravel's treasure,
handled with respect for its threat.

My brother caught fire burning trash.
I rolled him in the gravel
then picked diamonds from his scorched jacket,

grateful to have him whole,
grateful that God required
no burnt offering that day.

Bijou

Grandpa plucked the fruit of his money tree
every Saturday morning from June to September.
He gave us each a quarter and a nickel.
With cold, hard cash in our sweaty summer fists
we walked to the matinee on Main Street
for a twenty-five cent ticket
to sit and see
a double feature, three cartoons, the newsreel, previews
and the next installment of Jungle Boy's serial adventures.
The Bijou was dark and cool.
It smelled of popcorn
and farmers' kids in town for the day,
still itchy from picking cucumbers,
still scented from play in haylofts.
Our other five cents bought Jujubes, the dentist's delight
or Snow Caps that Grandma said would give us acne.
I always bought Jujubes
because the word went with Bijou.
I wondered what a *bijou* was.
A magic word like Ali Baba's *Sesame*
or Captain America's *Shazam?*
I tried the incantation,
nothing happened.
No, Bijou was a place,
a kingdom of mystery
where a wizard in the projection booth
whisked us from Seaforth, Ontario
to a U.S.A. boot camp with *Francis the Talking Mule.*
We danced in the rain with Gene Kelly,
swam with Esther Williams
and learned Weismuller's ape-man yell,

though it took hours of practice
in Grandma's canning kitchen to perfect it.
We time traveled from Hopalong Cassidy's dusty trails
to Buck Roger's space flights.
The Bijou was my heart's homeland
from reel to shining reel.

Your Money's Worth

The thirteen-cent goldfish died
of overindulgence.
He floated belly-up,
still amazed at an overabundance
he couldn't resist.

I have seen people on cruise ships
come close to that same expression,
floating into port
glazed as suckling pigs.

All-Inclusive is a deceptively
dangerous phrase.
Do you think it means
"Welcome to my country club?"
No, it's, "Get your money's worth."

Hit the breakfast buffet,
the mid-morning grill by the pool,
the pizza/bistro lunch,
afternoon tea with buttered scones,
and select at least one item
from each of the five courses for dinner,
then the midnight chocolate extravaganza.

You have paid for it all.
And you will pay again later.
Ask the fish.

Singin' the Fat Blues

I jiggle like a jello
       every time I take a walk.
My belly feels like jelly
       every time I take a walk.
I said I'd tuck my tummy, but Honey,
All I do is talk.

My clothes are getting smaller,
       my pants are splittin' at the seams.
Must be shrinkin' in the drier,
       my pants are splittin' at the seams.
I need a brand new wardrobe—
One of those Lane Bryant dreams.

So pass the carrots, Honey, the celery sticks
       and soybean beef.
I'm eatin' carrots, Honey, and celery sticks
       and soybean beef.
Don't show me the dessert tray,
That whipped cream only brings me grief.

I've made a resolution,
       cross my heart and hope to die.
I've made a resolution
       to shut my mouth and don't eat pie.
I'm goin' to lose this blubber,
       at least I'm goin' to truly try.
Oh my.

Sin Eater

She swallowed my troubles whole.
Do not chew sin, she advised.
The sweetness will close your throat,

What flavor is that star?

I stared at the birthmark of fear on her face
and told her that Orion's belt
was ripened peaches.

Pick one for me, she sang.

She named flowers.
I brewed tea from fallen petals.

Bronchial Etude

As I lie and listen to my bronchial tubes
pop and fizzle
and whistle like a two-year-old with a penny flute,
I wonder how to notate
the natural music of my body.
Rapid heartbeats
over-stimulated by anti-histamines
pulsate and pound with a rhythm
that shakes the cup of herbal tea
balancing on my belly
and sends calming chamomile
sloshing to the saucer in frenetic abandon.

Did you know that the fourth movement
of Beethoven's Second Symphony
was inspired by his indigestion?
Gurgles and gastric explosions,
hiccups and flatulence translated
into concert hall fare.
Mahler's Ninth is a musical rendition
of his heart's arrhythmia, coronary fibrillation,
fatal infarction
and subsequent funeral march.

Surely my chamber music
could be equally grand.
I moan in frustration
and hear oboes.

Playing Chopsticks

My mother had six children
and all of them knew how to play Chopsticks.
She considered it the pianist's rite of initiation.
If a kid had any keyboard talent at all
it would show up in that classic,
two-fingered, spinet-banging piece
with the inscrutable oriental name.
Dynamics, interpretation, and gusto
were noted as indications that piano lessons
might be a worthy investment.
But if your living room recital lacked luster,
you never even made it to Thompson's Book One.
I actually made it to Thompson's Book Two
though it took me three years of lessons
with Sister Angela Therese,
who did not have the patience of a saint
but was required by her vow of obedience
to drill little Catholics in scales and finger positions.
It was Purgatory all around.
Mother finally decide that my Chopsticks
had been a flash in the wok.
I was permitted to abandon all hope of a concert career
and take up tap dancing.
I was free to *Shuffle off to Buffalo*
and listen to my sisters
play Chopsticks.

She Marches to a Different Drummer

My grandma does not have white hair,
nope, hers is curly red.
Some grandmas knit and watch the soaps,
mine plays blackjack instead.
She's very good with numbers
and speaks a little French.
She has a tool kit in her car
with a pearl-handled wrench.
My grandma has a Ph.D.
My grandpa calls her Doc.
He taught her how to sail a boat
and how to leverage stock.
So if your grannie toes the line
that's fine, I'm not the judge,
but mine may win a Nobel Prize
while yours is making fudge.

My Study Is a Mess

There is no uncovered surface
       and none of my stuff is   junk.
           At one point   I attempted an ordering
by sorting things   into wicker baskets
and,   I am ashamed to admit it
       plastic bins and a few   canvas bags.
I have brought in two   collapsible   T.V. tables,
       but I never collapse them
because I need them   for my computer
          and unread literary journals
          which are stacked separately from
     all other forms   of unread literature.
Recently, I have resorted to Rubbermaid   tubs
       for larger collections and more ambitious projects,
          the kind that requires a lot of mulling.
I do not put lids on these tubs
         so my possibilities can breathe.
          I used to be not such a saver
until I started to forget   too much.
Now, if I can't bring something to   mind
      I go find the paper where I wrote it down
         if I can remember where I put it.
I take vitamins and go   for long walks
     in the hope   of staving off   dementia.
If I lose my mind
         it will be somewhere in my study.

Cup of Home

In the middle of the afternoon
I walk to the coffee shop,
order a cappuccino,
feel decadent, frivolous, yuppy.
Man, I love that caffeine,
love the foam, love the feel of the cup.
When my sister was in the Peace Corps
living in a thatched hut
without plumbing or electricity,
we mailed her Starbuck's coffee beans.
She had a battery-operated grinder
so she could start her days of frustration
and funerals with a cup of home.
I don't know how she lived
through spider bites and dysentery,
the Christmas goat slaughter,
Basotho males' domination of women,
the droughts and lightning strikes,
but I suspect coffee
had something to do with it.

Wordless

I woke up this morning
and didn't know how to write.
The alphabet, phonics, and all of Dr. Dolch's word lists
had seeped out of the sieve of my memory.
Dick and Jane and Spot and Puff
had stolen away in the night.
I saw marks on pages
and found them cryptic, decorative
but not enlightening.
I picked up a pencil,
sketched circles and sticks,
practiced the connected loops of Palmer's warm-up
and the classic slant of D'Nealian,
graceful but unintelligible.
Longing for the caves of Lascaux
and the brotherhood of hand-tracers,
I made a grocery list:
circles for oranges, ovals for eggs,
a rectangle with a wisp for a carton of Camels.
I did not go to the store.
How would I sign the credit slip at check-out?
Perhaps I would starve.
By noon I was mourning the loss of literacy
as one mourns the death of a lover.
I ate Hershey bars
and drank scotch out of the bottle.
I fell asleep on the couch
with chocolate on my chin
and a fifth of Johnny Walker
clasped to my bosom.

I dreamed of Descartes in a donkey cart.
He sang, "I think; therefore, I am."
I sang back, "I write; therefore, I think."
He did not laugh.
I woke up
and wrote this.

About the Author

Born in Detroit, Pat Barnes rejoices in the city's continuing renewal with its lively communities of artists, writers, storytellers, puppeteers and musicians.

Pat is a visual artist as well as a poet. She recognizes that just as an artist is constantly on the lookout for some representation of an object that can be a symbol of something richer than itself when it is put in partnership or conflict with another, so a poet manipulates language to juxtapose images in the hope of finding insight into . . . well, anything at all.

Pat lives in Wyandotte, Michigan where she is an active member of Springfed Arts, The Poetry Society of Michigan, and Downriver Poets and Playwrights.

Made in the USA
Lexington, KY
10 November 2019